T0105614

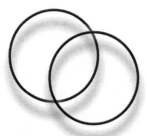

So You Want to Get Married?

A Quick Guide to Help You Choose the Right Spouse

Nick Sanchez

WestBow
PRESS
A DIVISION OF THOMAS NELSON

Nick Sanchez
SoYouWanttoGetMarried@aol.com

Front Cover Image, Emily Chastain Photography Copyright

Copyright © 2013 Nick Sanchez.

All rights reserved. No part of this book may be used or reproduced by any means, graphic, electronic, or mechanical, including photocopying, recording, taping or by any information storage retrieval system without the written permission of the publisher except in the case of brief quotations embodied in critical articles and reviews.

WestBow Press books may be ordered through booksellers or by contacting:

WestBow Press
A Division of Thomas Nelson
1663 Liberty Drive
Bloomington, IN 47403
www.westbowpress.com
1-(866) 928-1240

Because of the dynamic nature of the Internet, any web addresses or links contained in this book may have changed since publication and may no longer be valid. The views expressed in this work are solely those of the author and do not necessarily reflect the views of the publisher, and the publisher hereby disclaims any responsibility for them.

Any people depicted in stock imagery provided by Thinkstock are models, and such images are being used for illustrative purposes only.

Certain stock imagery © Thinkstock.

ISBN: 978-1-4497-8373-0 (sc)
ISBN: 978-1-4497-8374-7 (e)

Library of Congress Control Number: 2013902078

Printed in the United States of America

WestBow Press rev. date: 3/5/2013

Contents

Introduction ix

Is He the Right One? 1

Look at the Hand! 3

The Thumb—Core Ethics and Values 5

The Index (Pointer) Finger—Direction, Goals, and Ambition 13

The Middle Finger – Baggage and Problems 17

The Ring Finger – Family Values 25

The Pinky Finger – Physical Body Characteristics 33

Conclusion 39

Review Sheet 43

About the Author 49

Acknowledgments

I want to thank my wife and six children for having confidence in my ideas for this booklet and for encouraging me to write it. I could not have done it without their love, inspiration, and help throughout the entire process. I also wish to thank the many friends and family members who so willingly read and made suggestions to improve it.

Introduction

Do you feel scared or nervous when you think about whom you will marry, fearing that you could make a mistake? Marrying the wrong person could consume years of your life in pain and suffering, and ultimately break up your marriage. Divorce is running rampant, and its destructive tentacles have touched all of our lives in some way or another. Rest assured, however, that you can greatly increase your chances for a great and happy marriage by earnestly getting to know and understand those you date and befriend. Through prayer, self-reliance, and thoughtful assessment of your potential spouse, you can better prepare yourself for marriage.

Married life is sometimes hard. Everyone knows that it is full of challenges and unexpected twists and turns, and that everyone gets their share of them. To the surprise of many, a lot of the suffering associated with failed marriages *can* be prevented. Many people could tell you that they saw the telling signs of the cause of their failed marriage before they got married, but did not heed them at the time. Wouldn't it be great if people could openly talk about these signs in order to help those considering marriage avoid problems? This is precisely the purpose of this booklet.

Many good, solid, and successful marriages exist because the couples knew up front what they were getting into and accepted the required level of commitment, or they overcame their challenges through faith, hard work, dedication, and sacrifice. Marriage demands an individual's best efforts and eventually tests a couple's commitment in multiple ways. This is why it is critical for you to have a good picture of *who* this person is to whom you will be committing.

What I invite you to consider in the following pages will heighten your awareness of your prospect's strengths and weaknesses and how they could possibly impact your future and your family's future. These ideas can help you make critical relationship decisions with confidence, allowing you to move forward and make commitments or giving you the courage to discontinue a relationship if necessary.

I frankly and openly discuss five critical areas of a person's life, which you need to seriously explore before committing to a potential spouse. I want to help you so that as you meet individuals and begin to develop relationships, you will know what key things to look for.

I have written as if I were speaking to one of my own daughters and ask that you consider these ideas in the spirit of hearing fatherly advice. My intent is mostly to write to young women. However, these guidelines and principles apply to anyone, male or female, young or old, single, divorced, or widowed - anyone who is considering marriage.

Is He the Right One?

When several of our children were of dating age, I was asked by one of my eldest daughters, "Dad, how will I know if the guy I am dating is the *right one* to marry?" It was a moment when I was caught off guard, and time stood still for me. I realized that my kids had grown up. I had other growing sons and daughters and knew that eventually they too would ask me, or themselves, the same question. I do not recall what answer I gave at that time, but I do remember that for the following days the question lingered in my mind. As a concerned and loving father, I wanted to ensure I taught my children how to answer this important question for themselves since I may not always be around to address it.

By what I call inspiration, I came up with a simple set of ideas, which I now present as I originally taught them to my sons and daughters. It was not my intent to create an in-depth psychological or analytical dissertation for my kids on what love is or how to choose your spouse. Rather, I wanted this to be an informal, down-to-earth chat, evoking a friendly dialogue that a father, brother, grandfather, or close friend might have with a loved one who is looking for guidance about marriage.

I personally believe that marriage is the *second* most important decision anybody will make—yes, second only to whether one

will live a life of faith and obedience to God, or follow the ways of the world.

Many young people believe that more importance should be given to issues such as what school to go to, what career to pursue, or even where to live. Unfortunately, as important as these other decisions might seem, choosing the right spouse and having a successful marriage will do more for your happiness and future than anything else. So, it is critical that you choose well. Remember that your happiness is worth the patience and hard work required to achieve a good marriage. There are many who love you and who will also find great joy in your good decisions and strong family.

I hope this booklet will help you choose the *right one* and launch you into a new stage in life of joy, growth, and happiness—a successful marriage.

Notes:

_____

_____

_____

_____

_____

_____

_____

Look at the Hand!

$\mathcal{S}$oon after my father-to-daughter chat, I finalized the guide that would help my daughter remember key questions she needed to ask about the person she was dating. I wanted something that was easy for anybody to remember and apply—nothing cumbersome or complicated. I also wanted my daughter to be able to use the guide right there and then—during a date as she spoke and interacted with the young man. In my mind I pictured her and the young man holding hands and staring into each other's eyes—and then sheepishly looking down at their hands—you know, something that all young couples do. I wanted my daughter to have the tools to immediately focus on the more important things about him. The hand-holding would be at the heart of the equation because everyone usually holds hands to show affection early in a relationship.

Here is where inspiration about the hand-holding came to

me. I said to myself, "Look at the hand! Use the five fingers of the young man's hand and have her associate each one of them with the five most important things she needs to know about him." I had it! I knew it would work. The idea to use the fingers of the hand was the key to the whole process. I already knew the serious topics I wanted to discuss with her, so I simply associated them and their relative importance with each of the five fingers.

So, when your boyfriend (or girlfriend, if you're male) holds your hand, look at his hand and look at each specific finger to remember the ideas and questions you need to ask about him. *Each finger will represent a specific area about his life that you will absolutely need to know and explore before making a commitment of marriage.* So, just go from finger to finger considering the five specific points discussed in the following chapters. Doing so will begin to open up a view in your mind of what your future together would really look like. With this easy system, you will get a good feel as to whether this guy is a keeper! Look at the hand!

Notes:

_____

_____

_____

_____

_____

_____

_____

The Thumb—Core Ethics and Values

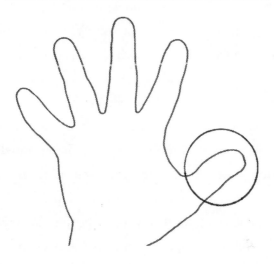

As you look at his hand to analyze him, begin by considering the thumb. Think of the thumb as being representative of what his *Core Ethics and Values* are.

It should represent the important things upon which he bases and anchors his life. Hopefully, what he considers important *runs in parallel and is similar to your core beliefs and values.* They should be those things that are of highest importance and priority to both you and him. If they are not, you need to reassess your relationship with him.

Core ethics and values represent spiritual and fundamental things that motivate your daily actions and form the basis of your character. So, why compare this critical question to the thumb?

Because of the powerful importance the thumb plays within the hand.

Let me explain something about the thumb. When a hand is missing the thumb, it becomes weak and is limited in utility and power. Even those things it can do without the use of the thumb are hard and cumbersome to accomplish. Without the thumb, it is hard to grasp and use tools such as hammers, pliers, screwdrivers, weapons, or many other tools. It is hard to do just about any kind of work requiring the hand. If you do not believe this, tape your thumb to your hand for a day, or even an hour, and see how many things you can do well without it. You will be surprised!

Working with sophisticated instruments that require the dexterity, the finesse, and the strength of the hand becomes complicated and compromised without the thumb. In real life, an individual's ability to work efficiently and provide for a family is severely hampered with an injured or weak hand with no thumb. I once heard that certain armies and workforces in the world do not allow a person without a thumb to join their ranks. Can you see why?

In marriage it is the same when the husband and wife do not have the same core ethics and values. If he believes very differently than you do, he will be like a *thumbless* hand to your marriage—severely hampering it. It is hard for any husband to provide true family leadership and guidance in the home without similar ethics and values. His sacred role as a husband and father cannot be fully developed and met because both of you will look at things differently. The supreme role of husbands, fathers, wives, and mothers is to use their core ethics and values as the platform or infrastructure to loving, raising, teaching, and supporting their family. It is hard to do this when such ethics and values do not exist or they are completely different.

You might ask, "What are core ethics and values?" Let me briefly say that they are a code, principles, or standards that you live by daily. They are what you consider good, bad, correct, incorrect, acceptable, unacceptable, or moral within your life and society. They could also be considered worthy, important, or desirable principles by a society.

An absence of such important principles within the head of a home can eventually impact a family's ability to survive times of trouble, challenge, and testing. Without a father's moral leadership, a family or a family member can more easily succumb to the unrelenting temptations and pressures of today's vice-ridden society. On the other hand, when a father provides ethical direction, instruction, and strength within the family, even the most challenging and difficult circumstances can be faced head-on with resolve.

If ethics and values are not the same for both of you, and they do not form the nucleus of your family upbringing, chances are that your family will eventually evolve into just another group of individuals emotionally tossed around by conflicting philosophies—quickly being subject to the many dangers that worldly lifestyles bring. This is what spouses and parents want to avoid.

Be aware that you are setting yourself up for major turmoil in your relationship and marriage if you move into a relationship where you don't share values with your boyfriend. This is why this point is so critical in moving forward in your commitment and relationship.

If we have committed our lives to living God's commandments, then the scriptures say that we are a peculiar people. As such, we have an obligation and a stewardship to be loving, respectful, and ethical to all creations—especially our families. And to be peculiar, our households need to be guided by high moral ethics and values. If not, husbands and fathers are left to guide and direct their families through their own philosophies, devices, wisdom, and worldly understanding, and the family members soon get lost in the sea of worldly ideas and suffer for it. I say this because just as the world is filled with great, beautiful, and incredible things, it too is riddled with immoral teachings, limited wisdom, and false ideas that can lead to a false sense of the purpose of life. No matter how *good* a person may otherwise seem, a lack of core ethics and values eventually leads a person (and consequently, a family) off the *straight and narrow* path of joy into sadness, emptiness, and suffering. It is just an inevitable result of not understanding the true purpose of life.

To avoid this, it is critical that you take the time to ask yourself the following questions to see where you stand. More importantly, you need to ask them about your future spouse and seek out the answers to them.

Questions

1. Does he have a strong belief in:
    a. God, the Creator, a heavenly Father, or celestial power or light?

b. A code of ethics and values that are the same as yours?

c. Respect for all life and the things you believe in and do?

d. Unselfish service to others as an important and integral part of a fulfilling life?

e. Faith in a *higher source* for help and support in life as you do?

2. Does he pray, study sacred scriptures, fast, and attend church services often?

3. Does he have a love of God and is he committed to Him?

Analysis

These critical questions should form the foundation of your relationship. Based on the answers you get, you can proceed with confidence that your relationship will be built upon a solid ethical and spiritual foundation, or you can get out of the relationship. Remember that if you marry and have children, your spouse's ethics and spirituality will impact their spiritual and overall development. If the young man does not have an ethical and moral foundation, your happiness and success as a couple and family will be at risk. If you believe that he does have them, go a little farther and ask yourself one more question—how strong is his foundation? Will it weather the challenges, temptations, and adversity that inevitably come throughout life?

Any man, even one without ethics and values, has the ability to do and accomplish many things, even good things, but he will be limited in the scope of that which is required of a true father and husband. Such simple things as children, church preference and attendance, offering monetary contributions, keeping the Sabbath day holy, and even how and when to serve others, affect and impact the relationship and daily family life. Without the same beliefs, the relationship will most likely be built upon mundane ideals and moral standards, which may not be conducive to the couple moving forward in the same direction in life.

On the other hand, if the individual has the same ethics and moral values, then the family can be built upon solid and sound principles that will develop faith, love, and knowledge. This, in turn, will enable the family to maintain clear perspectives on the purpose of life, which will promote diligence, service, and a healthy family life. It will also form the moral fiber of the children as they are born and become part of the family.

Marriage can be compared to a pair of oxen yoked together. You always get the best results from the pair when both are pulling in the same direction. When each pulls at different times or in different directions, or when one pulls and the other does not, the work is terribly hindered and not much is accomplished. In a marriage, the couple is similarly *yoked* together in a great cause called raising a family. If both have the same ethics and are of the same mind and spirit, you will be able to work and teach by word and example— together and harmoniously. Life is rewarding and exciting as you grow together and raise your family in love under these conditions.

Do not be impatient as you get to know your potential spouse. It will take time to be able to answer all of the questions about him with some kind of assurance. It is difficult to meet someone and within a week or even a few months be able to know much about the individual. Why? Because understanding the mind and heart of someone else is complex, and it takes more than occasional dates and spare time activities to really get to know someone. And it does not help that we all try to be our best to impress someone we like. Eventually, however, we all let our guards down, and we let people see us for who we really are. It takes time to get to know someone well.

We all know, or have heard, of couples who met and got engaged within a week and got married and are still married after seventy-five years, but they are one in a million, and such an approach is risky! You have to see the individual under the light of many different situations to truly see who he is. You have to see how he responds to being around his and your family. You need to witness how he reacts under circumstances and conditions at work, play, church, in social environments, and around other women, men, and children. A happy and successful future for you and your family may depend on this. It is always wise to make and take the time to get to know each other better. Physical kindness, care, and respect should form part of the relationship now. But physical intimacy is sacred and should always be reserved for marriage.

Though we know perfection is not achievable in this life, you do want to know if your future husband is sincerely striving for personal growth and improvement in his life. Here are some final questions for this section.

- Is his love for God evident and true and similar to yours?
- Does he have a proud heart that does not allow him to be humble, to be led by God, or to ask for forgiveness when he does something wrong?

- Is he service-oriented or is he self-centered, always expecting others to serve him?

A proud heart cannot feel the promptings of God, so when an individual is constantly thinking of why the world isn't watching him or attending to his needs, that can be a red flag of major concern for a budding relationship.

There is nothing else that will impact your marriage more than whether or not you both have the same core ethics, values, faith, and beliefs and whether you are both committed to living them. With that said, how does his thumb look?

Notes:

_____

_____

_____

_____

_____

_____

_____

The Index (Pointer) Finger—
Direction, Goals, and Ambition

*T*he next important finger on the hand you need to think about is the pointer finger (a.k.a. the index finger). This finger represents *the young man's direction in life, his goals and ambitions*. What direction is he pointing towards?

As you consider the person you are with, it is essential that you understand clearly what he wants to do in life and the steps he is now taking to achieve those goals. You never want to assume or guess what his goals are or what he wants to become. You have to know! There will come a time in his life when he will become the head of a family, a father, and a husband, and he will have to work to make a living. If you are to become his wife, you should have an understanding of what he is to become so that you feel comfortable as you both head in the same direction.

Perhaps, if he is a young student, he may not yet know exactly what he'll do for a living, but you can learn about his inclinations and aspirations. Does he talk about becoming an engineer, an administrator, a teacher, a plumber, an entrepreneur, or a musician? *More importantly, you need to know if he is a hard worker.* Being a hard worker will break or make any family! Is he taking the classes or necessary steps that will get him where he wants to go? Or is he just cruising, satisfied with part-time jobs or easy classes? Is he focused simply on having fun? You need to know.

Ask yourself the following questions about him and see if you know the answers.

Questions

1. What general direction in life is he pointing or heading to through his current actions?
2. Is the career direction he is heading toward going to provide adequately for your family, or will you struggle financially?
3. Does he have a plan for supporting a family? Has he discussed it with you?
4. Is he pursuing higher or advanced education or career training?
5. What are his goals and aspirations for the future? Have you discussed them with him?

6. Does he have a good work ethic and good work habits? What motivates him? Is he lazy?

7. Do you see him making real effort and real sacrifices to achieve the goals he says he has?

Analysis

The answers to these questions are extremely important because once you are married to him, you have committed your life to him and will live with the consequences. Know now where he is headed, and decide if that is the place where you want to end up. When you discuss these things with him, make sure that he is not just talking *pie in the sky* and telling you all types of things that sound *cool* or that you want to hear. You should feel comfortable and witness (see by his actions and not talk) that he is willing to work for what he is talking about. Many young men are still naïve and talk big about becoming great achievers, but do not know the complexities of how to achieve things they want or are unwilling to pay the price. You need to see that he is putting effort into becoming what he wants to become. If he is serious about it, you will see dedication and sacrifice, and you will see him giving his best efforts to doing well in whatever he does—consistently.

It is very important that a young man pursue the necessary education and have sound work ethics to achieve his goals. Survival in today's work force demands it, and more and more it is essential to provide for a family's needs and survival.

You will suffer if he is the type of person who will not or cannot hold down a job, who just sits at home and watches TV or plays videos games, all this while you have to leave your children and get a job to provide for the family. Remember, financial obligations are relentless and never-ending! You may think to yourself, "But he's a good guy!" Is he really a good guy? Ask yourself this critical question, *What is he good for?* You need to know. It's not just a cliché. Playing video games and/or watching TV or sports will not qualify him as a provider for your family. Remember, flowers and gifts and fancy restaurants during dating and courtship do not necessarily mean that he will be able to provide for a family. You cannot pay bills with *nice* alone.

Notes:

_____

_____

_____

_____

_____

_____

The Middle Finger —
Baggage and Problems

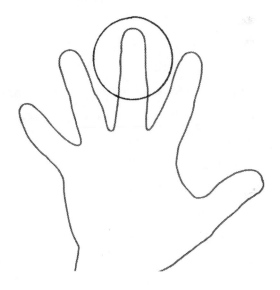

The next finger we will consider is the middle finger—a very interesting finger, to say the least.

We all have a history. Some of us call bad choices or events in our past our *skeletons in the closet*. I call this type of history *baggage*. As you consider your potential spouse, you need to keep your *eyes wide open* and seriously think about this finger and its implications. Think of the middle finger as the *bad finger*. Think of the possible *negative baggage that the individual might have now and in his past that could adversely impact your marriage and future family.*

By negative baggage I mean bad habits, weaknesses, past adverse situations, former marriages or serious relationships, and issues that could negatively affect your marriage and family down the road.

We all carry our problems as baggage, and we take them everywhere we go. It is something that we carry in our hearts, our thoughts, and even on our bodies. Some of us may carry a little tote bag that has hardly anything in it! But some of us are going around hauling a ten-piece set of baggage on roller wheels, jam packed with problems and heavy with serious pain-creating issues. You need to determine how much and what type of baggage he is hauling behind him and how he copes with it. Remember, once married to him, it becomes your baggage as well. You will have to haul it around everywhere you go—however painful and heavy it may be and whether you want to or not.

If you discover the individual you are dating has some serious issues, and you have an impulse or desire to help *"save"* him from his problems – *refrain! Marriage is not the way to do it.*

We should always encourage, support and help others, but remember, only they can *change* themselves! Marriage comes with its own challenges. Trying to "fix" someone through marriage is the wrong reason to marry and does not usually work.

Do *not* go into marriage or a relationship believing or thinking, "I can help him change," or "He will change with my example, my love, and my efforts." Do not fall for the romantic belief that he'll change for you. In most cases he will *not* change, and misery and pain await the majority of those who enter marriage under these assumptions. Many times your heart will let you know if there is a serious issue here—be prepared to listen to that *small voice* or gut feeling and **act upon it!** Get out of the relationship now.

For such an important decision as marriage, you need to clearly assess the person's baggage and the dangers that it brings. Determine whether this is something you and your children will want to deal with for the rest of your lives. It is not enough to think that *you* can handle it; you must also think of the impact it will have on your future children. You must earnestly pray about it, and give it time, before you consider taking on a relationship burdened with dangerous baggage. Listen to the Spirit and follow its promptings. You will never regret it! Remember, marriage is a serious commitment where you take on each other's baggage. All of us have some kind of baggage in our lives, and this is not an impediment to a successful marriage. The key question you need to ask is, What is his baggage, how has he dealt with it, and am I committed to hauling it around?

Note for Christians: I believe in the cleansing power of true repentance through the atonement of Jesus Christ. We can turn away from the bad we are doing and go the opposite direction, never to do the bad again, and allow the atonement to cleanse us. Therefore, be cautious and thoughtful about a person's past, repented-of sins, or transgressions. Through the atonement of Jesus Christ, people can and do change! Be extremely sensitive about discussing those things for which you or your potential spouse have fully and completely repented. At the same time, it is important to know about those issues that could bring challenges to a marriage—things like addictions, previous marriages, or issues with pornography, anger or violence, or drugs. Even though these things may be in the past, they are pesky and can and do often return and affect the relationship. They must be openly and carefully considered before marriage. Unrepented-of sins and other shortcomings should be the focus of the middle-finger analysis. What does his baggage look like to you?

Begin this process by asking yourself the following questions about your intended spouse:

Questions

1. What specifically have I identified as his baggage? Write down potential issues, number them, describe the problems, and analyze them.
2. Is he normally happy or emotionally dark, depressed, and closed? Why is he so? You need to know!
3. How does he deal with adversity, challenges, or life's hang-ups—with anger, drugs, alcohol, and denial?
4. Is he vindictive, aggressive, or emotionally unstable?
5. Is he a grateful person, or does he take things for granted and feel the world revolves around him?

Analysis

Any baggage impacts and affects immediate and future family

relationships deeply. Heavy-duty baggage can include things like:

out-of-wedlock children	laziness/idleness
excessive/credit card debt	cheating
verbal and physical abuse	drug and/or alcohol use or addiction
pornography	association with cults
gambling	unfaithfulness
divorce	addictive spending
trouble with the law	mental disorders
trouble with the church	sin
gang activity	dishonesty
stealing	children from previous relationship
lying	anger issues

The list is endless, and these things cause more misery and pain in marriages than you can imagine. These are also the types of things we do not want people to know about us, and we'll hide them or play them down. So it is important that you openly and courageously discuss these topics if you sense there is a problem. Learn about his background and get a sound understanding of who he really is. Your instinct and the still small voice within you can guide and direct you—listen to it! Do not be afraid! Have the courage to drop the relationship now if prompted to do so. Talk to your family, friends, or spiritual leaders if you need support.

It is essential that you know these things early on because in many cases they are only revealed months or years later when you are already married. Here again, it is wise to take the time to get to know the person thoroughly before you make the commitment to marriage.

Time allows you to find out about him from friends, family, and from your own personal interaction with him. It is like doing a triangulation from three different satellites in space to determine the true location of a point on the earth. We can usually find out true facts about a person by hearing from three different and distinct sources. You need to have multiple witnesses telling you about who this person really is.

Do not look for perfect people to marry—because there are none! Tolerance, forgiveness, patience, growth, and development are always part of a marriage. However, some people have serious character flaws or other problematic issues that could lead to painful difficulties. Rest assured that if you rely on your instinct, your gut feeling, or that *still small voice* within you, you can find someone to love who will bring you joy and the best chance of achieving a happy, fulfilling, and successful marriage. Remember, you must be aware of and committed to his baggage.

Notes:

_____

_____

_____

_____

_____

_____

_____

The Ring Finger — Family Values

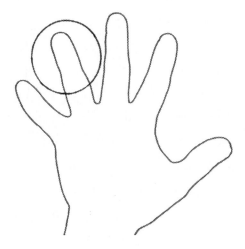

The next finger in line is the ring finger. This finger is where the wedding band goes, and it represents one of the most influential aspects of an individual's life—his family values! It encompasses all that a marriage represents and reflects the family he comes from and the family he desires.

When you think of the ring finger, think about what it stands for. This finger *should represent the family values he brings to the marriage—including chastity, loyalty, and fidelity.*

To know what family values he has, you must observe his social interactions with his own family and others. Whenever possible, make it a point to spend time with his parents, siblings, and extended family. Try to get a sense of the parents' relationship and how they treat each other. Be aware of the strengths and weaknesses they have in their relationship. Observe the siblings and even the extended family members, if you get a chance. Do you see love and respect between them, or do you see disrespect, disloyalty, and indifference among them? Do you feel or sense joy and happiness when you're with them?

The powerful influence of one's family life can never be overlooked. Family vices take tolls on various aspects of a child's habits, self-perception, respect for others, and life course. Your boyfriend *has* been influenced deeply by his family—or lack thereof. It is your responsibility to find out how. If you are not in a position to meet with his family, pay special attention whenever he speaks to his parents on the phone or by other means of communication. Take note when he talks about family members. If he doesn't talk about family members, ask him about them. It is critical that you know something about his family. As you meet and get to know him and his family, ask yourself these questions about the ring finger and his family values.

Questions

1. Can you name five important family values that he has? Write them down and ponder them. If you cannot, there may be a problem.
2. What kind of relationship does he have with his parents and siblings?
3. What importance does family have for him?

4. Does he honor and respect his parents and women in general?

Analysis

No person chooses the type of family or circumstances into which he will be born. We could have been born into a rich or royal family, or just as easily into a poor and destitute one. We could have been born into a spiritual and loving family, or into a spiritually and emotionally broken-down one. We could have come from an atheist family, or from a religious, scientific, or agnostic one. The point is that we cannot control where we come from, but we can control with whom we choose to spend our lives. We cannot change the circumstances of our birth and childhood, but with the knowledge and opportunities we have, all of us can choose to act upon what we have been given and improve our lives. It is important to note that some of us are innocent victims of adverse circumstances, and through no choice of ours, become entangled in some serious painful problems and issues. A *power from on high* is the only thing that can truly rescue us from such problems. Meanwhile, we can make right choices in life that can break us away from the shackles and chains of old habits and destructive, dysfunctional family patterns.

Make sure that your potential spouse has a good understanding of where he came from and where he is going when it comes to the family. Whatever family experiences he has, he will most likely bring into your family and will impact how your family will be raised.

Recognize that this aspect of your boyfriend's life may be a great strength as well. It is a powerful thing for a young man to grow up in a home where his father loves and honors his wife; where siblings are true friends and love one another; and where faith, hard work, and talents were fostered. You and your children can be the beneficiaries of his family's strengths.

The ideal is for all of us to have been born into a family where the spirit of God dwelt and where our parents had family-based wholesome activities—a home where our mothers and fathers taught us faith, respect, integrity, kindness, honesty, work, service, and love. Since for some of us this will not be the case, just remember that the strengths and/or weaknesses that your potential husband has in his family will most likely be brought into your future family. You want to make sure you are committed to that.

I know a young man whose parents had a rocky relationship. They finally divorced while he was on his church mission. It was a difficult time for him, and he wondered whether he would be able to have a successful marriage afterward. A loving church leader gave him wise counsel by telling him that his future family relationships could be whatever *he* chose them to be. If he followed God's teachings and chose each day to love and appreciate his spouse, he could have a very happy and healthy marriage.

The young man returned from his mission and began to court a worthy young daughter of God. They were married and have an extraordinarily happy marriage and family life with two beautiful children. Statistically, children who come from broken homes often follow in their parents' footsteps. However, this does not have to be the case. For that reason, a potential spouse's family is only one consideration to be weighed against all others. It is an important one, but is not absolute, in and of itself. You must know your boyfriend's family values, not just his family's family values.

As you will be joining one another's families, it is important that you feel comfortable with his family and that you are shown love and respect, and vice versa. The type of relationship and respect your boyfriend saw in his parent's marriage might be the same type of relationship he believes he needs to develop with you. The relationship he has with his siblings can also have a significant impact on the relationships he will expect with his children.

Loyalty and Fidelity

Other critical aspects of the ring finger with its family values are loyalty and fidelity. This entails the commitment and vigor with which he turns his heart over to you. How faithful will he be and remain to you? A professor of social work of a major USA university once said that there are different types of infidelity—physical and emotional—and that they are "an insidious threat that can weaken the trust between a couple and shatter peace of mind."[1] So as you think of your beau and all that he is, ask yourself about his physical and emotional loyalty to you. Will he allow infidelity to infiltrate and spoil your marriage?

We know through scripture that once we make a commitment to marry, all other individuals and/or relationships should take a secondary status in order of importance in our life—including mother and father. It says, "Therefore, shall a man leave his father and mother [and former girlfriends, might I add], and shall cleave

---

1   Ensign, *Fidelity in Marriage,* September 2009, p 14.

unto his wife: and they shall be one flesh."[2] There is a great power and love in a relationship where most sacred commitments of loyalty and fidelity have been made between the husband and wife. A renowned church leader said it perfectly when he warned,

> "There are those married people who permit their eyes to wander and their hearts to become vagrant, who think it is not improper to flirt a little, to share their hearts, and have desire for someone other than the wife or the husband. The Lord says in no uncertain terms: "Thou shalt love thy wife with all thy heart, and shalt cleave unto her and to none else."[3] And, when the Lord says *all thy heart*, it allows for no sharing nor dividing nor depriving. And, to the woman it is paraphrased: "Thou shalt love thy husband with all thy heart and shalt cleave unto him and none else." The words *none else* eliminate everyone and everything. The spouse then becomes preeminent in the life of the husband or wife, and neither social life nor occupational life nor political life nor any other interest nor person nor thing shall ever take precedence over the companion spouse."[4]

Your relationship with him is just beginning, so take the time to find out what his feelings are on commitment and fidelity.

---

2   Genesis 2:24

3   Doctrine and Covenants 42:22

4   Spencer W. Kimball, *Faith Precedes the Miracle* (1972), 142-43.

Listen to the promptings of the Spirit. It can guide and direct you as you assess your relationship. You can have a very good vision of what and who this young man is. You just need to be wise about it and not let love *blind* you. Do not be afraid to ask questions. How strong is his ring finger?

Questions

1. Does he know and understand the importance of fidelity in your relationship?
2. Is he the type of man that will be emotionally and physically faithful to you?
3. Are there old relationships in his life that have not been resolved that could impede your flourishing relationship?

Notes:

_____

_____

_____

_____

_____

_____

_____

The Pinky Finger — Physical Body Characteristics

The last finger of his hand I want to discuss is what is commonly called the pinky finger. It would seem that since it is the smallest and weakest of the fingers, it would be insignificant. However, it too plays an important role, *though not as important as the others. The pinky finger represents his physical characteristics—both external as well as internal.* By external I mean his looks—his hair, eyes, and body type, and whether you like him and are attracted to him. By the internal, I mean his health and family genes, which I will discuss more at length ahead.

This finger is like a two-edged sword. You can easily go

to extremes by either giving too much weight to the physical aspects of the individual or totally ignoring them or pretending there is no problem. I have witnessed some young ladies make a terrible mistake by considering physical characteristics the primary reason to marry someone. Some consider it only second in importance to his bank account and profession! They later end up divorced. In all seriousness, his physical characteristics should be considered of less importance than the issues covered previously with the first four fingers. And although it carries less weight in your decision making process, you should not ignore it either. You need to like him and be physically attracted to him because you will live with him for the rest of your life! He does not have to be the perfect creation of man, as Hollywood would make you believe, but you do want to like him and feel comfortable with him.

As far as the internal genes and health go, this is something you need to consider. Consider his family's history of medical issues (e.g., cancer, hemophilia, diabetes, or emotional or mental disorders). Just about every family has someone with these types of issues, so it is important that you *be aware of them* and evaluate their seriousness. Consider the impact they could have on you and your children. It's *not* a matter of judging or condemning the person, but of being aware of these problems, and making a commitment to accept and live with their potential implications, which in some cases may be difficult and challenging. Marriage can bring additional joy and happiness to an individual, as well as additional burdens, so you want to be aware of the burdens that his genes may bring into the picture.

I have known couples in which a person has chosen to marry someone with a serious disability or disease, and they have lived happily. In one couple's case, the woman was paralyzed from the hips down and was permanently in a wheelchair. Nonetheless, they got married, had several children, and lived happily. He accepted all the challenges and responsibilities that came with their circumstances and never complained about it. All the hardships that the situation brought, which cannot be understated, were difficult but surmountable. They were faced straight-on by the couple, since they both had committed to that type of relationship, and they had a great family. They were able to live as a family with a positive attitude and endured the difficulties and hardships with unconditional love throughout their lives.

I have also seen the opposite scenario in couples, where one of the two (or both) were not committed to the difficult circumstances, and they chose to ignore or lightly consider the complexities and difficulties, eventually resulting in divorce. You need to decide if the external and internal physical circumstances he brings could hinder your ability to live a happy, productive life. Remember, they will not change once the honeymoon is over, or even over many years.

To reduce the possibility of adding unnecessary burdens to your marriage, consider the following questions and make sure you know the answers:

Questions

1. Are you attracted to him and do you like his personality?
2. Are there hereditary illnesses, handicaps, and/or issues with

which you will need to live, and are you committed to live
with them?

3. Is he physically active, strong, able to work and provide for
his family, and does he live a healthy lifestyle?

4. Has he, in the past, and does he now, abstain from drugs and
alcohol, and does he eat healthy foods?

5. Can you commit to and live happily within the circumstances
of the relationship that cannot be changed?

Analysis

Some young women, desperate and afraid that they will be
left behind, will marry someone simply because he gives them the
attention or companionship they crave. They're even willing to
marry someone with obvious serious problems, or whom they do
not like at all, just to get married! What a mistake this turns out
to be. There are cases of women who have done this, who after
they've been married for a while realize they cannot continue *living
a lie* with a person they never *liked* and end up divorcing. Of
course, these cases can be remedied but require therapy, work,
and commitment. After some time, after the new marriage loses
its luster, they realize that they are not committed to live under
the conditions to which they initially agreed upon in their mind,
and then the serious problems surge. Are you prepared to live with
these problems or potential problems for the rest of your life? What
implications do these issues have for you ten years down the road?
Will you stand the test of time? Now is the time to choose.

None of us have perfect bodies. We are all subject to illness
and disease. Physical problems could come in the future, to either

you or your spouse, that were completely unforeseeable at the altar. So remember, this element of life is important and has long lasting implications. Your commitment should be strong enough in the other areas to overcome the unexpected frailties we are subject to in life.

Notes:

_____

_____

_____

_____

_____

_____

_____

Conclusion

The objective of this booklet has been to help you assess and make wise and intelligent decisions about whom you could marry.

I have purposefully omitted saying anything specific about *love* and what it means, or the role it plays in deciding to get married, but have instead focused on different types of practical issues typically excluded from conversations about marriage. The feelings of romantic love are important and do play a fundamental role in marriage, but this book is not about that. The points I have addressed are those many young women avoid because the questions are tough to address and answer, or because the young women are naïve and don't realize the implications. Hopefully this booklet will now make it easier for you to consider the hard questions. Read it multiple times; take notes about what you think and feel; pray about it; and don't be afraid to discuss the issues with your Mom and Dad and/or friends you trust. Use it as a "reality check" tool to enhance your understanding of your relationships.

Now, with that said, remember to also look at the good and positive things about him. Look for things he does well and how he focuses on improving himself. Be open to the things you like about him, but don't discard or minimize the importance of the five points discussed.

Fervent prayer, meditation, pondering, and reliance on God for guidance and confirmation about whom you will marry are important. Keep in mind that God will *not* choose for you! You must choose whom you will marry. God's role is only to confirm your choice, by either making you feel good, at peace, and confident about your decision, or making you feel uneasy, doubtful, and concerned.

If you feel troubled, confused, and sense that the young man is not right for you, *do not enter into the bonds of marriage!* Being nervous and scared is normal, but it is very different than feeling and knowing deep down inside, that something is wrong.

Bypassing inspiration in this decision could put your future family at risk. Remember the old advice given in Proverbs 3:4–5, which states, "Trust in the Lord with all thine heart; and lean not unto thine own understanding. In all thy ways acknowledge him, and *He shall direct thy paths*" (emphasis added). Relying solely on reason or your "feelings of love" is a dangerous chance you do not want to take. *Personal inspiration must be part of your decision.*

The life of an individual is very complicated, and one could never get to know everything about another person. However, relying on a higher power and knowing these five fundamental areas about a person can put you on the path to choosing and living a happy married life. You can leave aside most of the pain and suffering that many couples experience due to their lack of thoughtfulness in choosing the right spouse. An ancient American spiritual leader taught that "men [and women] are, that they might have joy."[5] Joy is a by-product of faith, knowledge, and

5   BoM, 2 Nephi 2:25

obedience to God's commandments. Marriage, with all of these ingredients, is perhaps the greatest way to experience true joy and happiness. Marriage is a commitment to spending your life as partners, and as such, requires that you know enough about the man to reasonably know what to expect from him in your married years.

As you get to know him better during your courtship, periodically review the five fingers and what they represent. Review the five areas with your friends to see how well you know him. Also, encourage your friends to "Look at the hand of their beau" when they start getting serious with someone.

When you look at your potential husband's hand, can you talk about what each of the fingers represents? If you can, then you are better prepared to make a decision about marriage with him.

Warning: There are no guarantees in life. You can choose to marry a worthy and wonderful companion with the same ethical foundations as yours, and he can in the future choose to make bad choices that can lead to sin, suffering, and divorce. You only have the power to do your part. So be patient, look carefully, have faith, choose wisely and keep God's commandments. Doing this will increase your chances for a successful marriage. You never fail when you choose to do what is right - regardless of what choices your spouse may make.

Review Sheet

The Thumb—This is the most powerful finger and it represents the core beliefs and values that he bases and anchors his life upon. It *should be the thing that is of the highest priority to him and should be the same or similar to yours.* Since this will form the spiritual infrastructure of your family, you want to ensure that you have a shared foundation of ethics and values upon which to build your family.

The Index Finger (pointing)—This finger represents his ambitions, goals, and the direction he is pointing to in life. This could very likely be the direction he will head towards with you and your family.

The Middle Finger—This finger represents the *baggage* he may be lugging around; it could be his bad history, habits, philosophies, or sin. Is your level of commitment sufficient to deal with his baggage for the rest of your life? Remember, his baggage becomes yours, and his baggage coupled with yours becomes your children's.

The Ring Finger—This finger represents his family background and values, his loyalty to you, and the physical and emotional fidelity he brings to your relationship. This will either bring immense joy and happiness to you or pain and suffering, depending on what his values are.

The Pinky Finger—This finger represents whether you are physically attracted and committed to him and whether there are any hereditary/health issues that may affect your family in the future. Be aware of what they are and be prepared to commit to them throughout your family life.

Mirror Analysis

Now look at yourself in the mirror—what do you see? If you expect a spiritual giant of a husband, be a spiritual giant of a wife. Whatever you expect of your partner, you too must reflect and expect of yourself. If you do not feel good about yourself and feel you are imperfect because of your past, fear not—move forward in faith with a plan to improve! Be willing to pull out of the relationship and take the necessary time to better and prepare yourself for the kind of commitment that marriage requires. Be what God and you require of yourself, and do not settle for less. Living your standards is more important than just getting married for the sake of being married. Be wise in your decisions.

Figuratively speaking, all of us have an imperfect hand. Some fingers may be mangled, scarred, broken, or even cut short or amputated, and marriage may still be the right choice. The key is being aware of and committed to the hand you choose to hold. Through God's power, all of our fingers can be made strong and whole again!

Marriage is the process through which we, as human beings, can experience the complete emotions of fulfillment and happiness in life. It is part of God's eternal plan through which single individuals progress to the next phase of life and partner with a spouse of the opposite sex to form the ultimate organization of the human race—a family.

In turn, families created under the sacred ordinance of marriage have the greatest potential to bring joy and happiness to their children and the world. Undoubtedly, the family, through loving parents, is the most influential place to prepare current and future generations of the human race for a peaceful and fulfilling existence. Not only are most people given the opportunity to naturally grow up in families, but they are also given the prospect to form their own families through marriage. If you follow these guidelines and respond to the inspiration from God, you will be better prepared to experience life to its fullest through your own successful marriage.

Feedback?

We would like to hear from you. Send us your feedback as to how you or your friends have put these principles to practice and the success you've had with them. Please send your feedback to: soyouwanttogetmarried@aol.com

Sources

Doctrine and Covenants, The Church of Jesus Christ of Latter-day Saints, Salt Lake City, Utah, 1981.

Ensign, Official publication of The Church of Jesus Christ of Latter-day Saints.

Holy Bible, Authorized King James Version with Explanatory Notes and Cross References to the Standard Works of The Church of Jesus Christ of Latter-day Saints. Salt Lake City; The Church of Jesus Christ of Latter-day Saints, 1979.

The Book of Mormon, Another Testament of Jesus Christ, The Church of Jesus Christ of Latter-day Saints, Salt Lake City, Utah, 1981.

About the Author

Nick Sanchez spent the majority of his career in the software sales industry, working with people in over twenty countries of Latin America, Europe, and North America. Born and raised in El Paso, Texas, he's had the unique opportunity to see the cause and effect of marriage decisions made by individuals from all socioeconomic levels and cultures. He has always had a passion for people and an interest in human nature, which was heightened by his undergraduate studies in English at Brigham Young University, Provo, Utah. He met his wife Marcela there and they have enjoyed a happy marriage for over thirty years. They are the parents of six children—five of whom are married, and now enjoy nine grandchildren. They currently reside in Colorado.

Printed in the United States
By Bookmasters